J j
B
RICHMOND.

D0883605

SPORTS GREAT MITCH RICHMOND

—*Sports Great Books*—

BASEBALL

Sports Great Jim Abbott
0-89490-395-0/ Savage

Sports Great Bobby Bonilla
0-89490-417-5/ Knapp

Sports Great Orel Hershiser
0-89490-389-6/ Knapp

Sports Great Bo Jackson
0-89490-281-4/ Knapp

Sports Great Greg Maddux
0-89490-873-1/ Thornley

Sports Great Kirby Puckett
0-89490-392-6/ Aaseng

Sports Great Cal Ripken, Jr.
0-89490-387-X/ Macnow

Sports Great Nolan Ryan
0-89490-394-2/ Lace

Sports Great Darryl Strawberry
0-89490-291-1/ Torres & Sullivan

BASKETBALL

Sports Great Charles Barkley
Revised Edition
0-7660-1004-X/ Macnow

Sports Great Larry Bird
0-89490-368-3/ Kavanagh

Sports Great Muggsy Bogues
0-89490-876-6/ Rekela

Sports Great Patrick Ewing
0-89490-369-1/ Kavanagh

Sports Great Anfernee Hardaway
0-89490-758-1/ Rekela

Sports Great Juwan Howard
0-7660-1065-1/ Savage

Sports Great Magic Johnson
Revised and Expanded
0-89490-348-9/ Haskins

Sports Great Michael Jordan
Revised Edition
0-89490-978-9/ Aaseng

Sports Great Jason Kidd
0-7660-1001-5/ Torres

Sports Great Karl Malone
0-89490-599-6/ Savage

Sports Great Reggie Miller
0-89490-874-X/ Thornley

Sports Great Alonzo Mourning
0-89490-875-8/ Fortunato

Sports Great Hakeem Olajuwon
0-89490-372-1/ Knapp

Sports Great Shaquille O'Neal
Revised Edition
0-7660-1003-1/ Sullivan

Sports Great Scottie Pippen
0-89490-755-7/ Bjarkman

Sports Great Mitch Richmond
0-7660-1070-8/ Grody

Sports Great David Robinson
Revised Edition
0-7660-1077-5/ Aaseng

Sports Great Dennis Rodman
0-89490-759-X/ Thornley

Sports Great John Stockton
0-89490-598-8/ Aaseng

Sports Great Isiah Thomas
0-89490-374-8/ Knapp

Sports Great Chris Webber
0-7660-1069-4/ Macnow

Sports Great Dominique Wilkins
0-89490-754-9/ Bjarkman

FOOTBALL

Sports Great Troy Aikman
0-89490-593-7/ Macnow

Sports Great Jerome Bettis
0-89490-872-3/ Majewski

Sports Great John Elway
0-89490-282-2/ Fox

Sports Great Brett Favre
0-7660-1000-7/ Savage

Sports Great Jim Kelly
0-89490-670-4/ Harrington

Sports Great Joe Montana
0-89490-371-3/ Kavanagh

Sports Great Jerry Rice
0-89490-419-1/ Dickey

Sports Great Barry Sanders
Revised Edition
0-7660-1067-8/ Knapp

Sports Great Deion Sanders
0-7660-1068-6/ Macnow

Sports Great Emmitt Smith
0-7660-1002-3/ Grabowski

Sports Great Herschel Walker
0-89490-207-5/ Benagh

OTHER

Sports Great Michael Chang
0-7660-1223-9/ Ditchfield

Sports Great Oscar De La Hoya
0-7660-1066-X/ Torres

Sports Great Steffi Graf
0-89490-597-X/ Knapp

Sports Great Wayne Gretzky
0-89490-757-3/ Rappoport

Sports Great Mario Lemieux
0-89490-596-1/ Knapp

Sports Great Eric Lindros
0-89490-871-5/ Rappoport

Sports Great Pete Sampras
0-89490-756-5/ Sherrow

SPORTS GREAT
MITCH
RICHMOND

Carl W. Grody

—Sports Great Books—

Enslow Publishers, Inc.

44 Fadem Road   PO Box 38
Box 699   Aldershot
Springfield, NJ 07081 Hants GU12 6BP
USA   UK
http://www.enslow.com

Dedication
To Kylee, who can probably read this book by now.

Library of Congress Cataloging-in-Publication Data

Grody, Carl W.
    Sports Great Mitch Richmond / Carl Grody.
        p. cm. — (Sports great books)
    Includes index.
    Summary: A biography of the All-Star guard and member of the United States basketball team that won a gold medal at the 1996 summer Olympics.
    ISBN 0-7660-1070-8
    1. Richmond, Mitch—Juvenile literature. 2. Basketball players—United States—Biography—Juvenile literature. [1. Richmond, Mitch. 2. Basketball players. 3. Afro-Americans—Biography.] I. Title. II. Series.
GV884.R53G67 1999
796.323'092
[B]—DC21
                                             98-13482
                                              CIP
                                              AC

Printed in the United States of America

10 9 8 7 6 5 4 3 2 1

To Our Readers:
All Internet addresses in this book were active and appropriate when we went to press. Any comments or suggestions can be sent by e-mail to Comments@enslow.com or to the address on the back cover.

Illustration Credits: Courtesy of Ernell O'Neal, pp. 14, 18, 30, 58; Kansas State Sports Information, pp. 22, 24, 27, 33; Property of Golden State Warriors, pp. 36, 39; Scott A. Kissell, pp. 8, 10, 11, 43, 48, 52, 54, 56, 59.

Cover Illustration: Scott A. Kissell

Contents

Acknowledgments

The author would like to thank the following people and organizations for their assistance: Ernell O'Neal; Dana Altman; Lon Kruger; Steve Henson; Jim Polk; Eric McDowell and the Golden State Warriors public relations department; Karen Washington of the NBA Players Association; Kansas State Sports Information Director Dan Wallenberg and his assistant, Krista Darding; the sports information departments at the University of Illinois, Creighton University, and Moberly Area Junior College; the New Jersey Nets public relations department; the administrative staff of Boyd Anderson High School in Fort Lauderdale, Florida; and Scott Kissell, who took many of the photos.

Chapter 1

Mitch Richmond entered the 1995 NBA All-Star Game as a forgotten man. Sure, the coaches and other players knew about Richmond, a shooting guard for the Sacramento Kings. But fans ignored him when choosing All-Star starters every year. Their votes went to big-name players in bigger cities.

Richmond entered that All-Star Game in Phoenix, Arizona, with something to prove. He didn't do much early in the game, making just one shot in the first quarter. But Richmond heated up in the second quarter.

He nailed a jumper from the left corner. He followed that with two lay-ups, then made a beautiful pass to Karl Malone for another bucket. When he left the game midway through the second period, Richmond's Western Conference All-Stars led the East, 53–39.

For a lot of players, that would've been enough. Richmond had 8 points in 12 minutes of action. With so many big-name players on the court, Richmond could have slipped away and nobody would've noticed.

Of course, Richmond was used to being overlooked. As a

Mitch Richmond (left) jokes around with fellow NBA All-Star Reggie Miller of the Indiana Pacers. Richmond and Miller are usually among the league's scoring leaders.

child, most of the attention went to his friend, Michael Irvin, who became a star wide receiver for the Dallas Cowboys. In college, Richmond played in the shadow of Danny Manning. In the NBA, Richmond was traded by his first team because it thought he was less valuable than his teammates.

But Richmond was not going to fade away. He returned to the All-Star Game halfway through the third quarter with the West leading, 79–67, and quickly took over. With 5:13 left in the quarter, he nailed a three-pointer. Forty-three seconds later, he made another jump shot. After the East's Grant Hill missed two free throws, Richmond threw in another jumper. Then, with just 21.8 seconds left in the quarter, Richmond drilled another three-pointer to give the West a 101–81 lead.

Richmond had scored 10 points in the period to help the

West pull away for the eventual 139–112 win. He finished the game with 22 points, 4 rebounds, and 2 assists. He made 10 of his 13 shots, including all 3 of his three-pointers. He was also named the game's Most Valuable Player.

"I've been watching this game for years," Richmond said after the game, "and you always dream of being up there [on the MVP podium], but it's just overwhelming."

Richmond's performance didn't surprise anyone who really knew basketball.

"He can shoot the ball," said Gary Payton, the point guard from the Seattle SuperSonics. "When he started filling it up, I just kept going to him. I'm glad he won [the MVP]. He's going to get some recognition now."

"Mitch plays like that all the time," said Phoenix Suns head coach Paul Westphal, who coached the West that day. "He's super."

Richmond is six-foot-five and powerful. He's one of the best shooters in the league. He guards the other team's top scoring guard. Coaches and fellow players rave about him.

He was one of only seven players in NBA history to average at least 21 points per game in each of his first nine seasons. He led all NBA guards in scoring twice. He was a member of Dream Team III. And he's one of the best defensive players in the league.

"He plays both ends of the court," said former teammate Chris Mullin. "He's not just an offensive player, not just a guy who goes for the glory. He does all the dirty work, too."

"He's very quietly become one of the best ever," said Lon Kruger, Richmond's head coach at Kansas State University.

Even Michael Jordan agrees. "Mitch's physical ability causes trouble both offensively and defensively," Jordan said. "I have a lot of respect for him. He's competition."

Being called competition by Jordan is like being named a

Concentrating on the basket, Mitch Richmond takes a foul shot. Richmond is known as one of the NBA's deadliest shooters.

saint by the Pope. It's the ultimate compliment, the brand of a truly great player. Yet his game has not caught on with national media and fans. As the Gatorade commercial said, everyone wants to "be like Mike." Why don't they want to be like Mitch?

One reason is that Richmond is too nice to demand attention. When he was left off the All-Star team in 1990, he didn't complain. When he was ignored for Dream Team II, he turned the other cheek. When he wasn't elected to the 1995 All-Star Game by the fans, he quietly accepted a spot as a reserve.

The second reason is that Richmond has played his entire career in small markets. He was a college star in Manhattan—Kansas, not New York City. His first NBA team was Golden State, which doesn't attract national reporters as New York, Chicago, and Los Angeles do. And then he was traded to

Having spent the bulk of his career on losing teams in Sacramento, Mitch Richmond has not gotten the recognition many feel he deserves.

Sacramento, which gets less attention than any other team in the league. In 1998, Richmond was traded to the Washington Wizards.

The third reason is that America loves winning teams. Jordan has won six championships with the Bulls. Richmond's Kings have never won half of their games, and they've only been in the playoffs once since 1986.

So when Richmond held the MVP trophy over his head after the 1995 All-Star Game, he could've used the spotlight to complain about being ignored. Instead, he said, "It hasn't been great playing in Sacramento the last few years because of our record, but this year I could come to the All-Star Game with my head up high and say with pride that I am a Sacramento King."

Earlier in the year, Richmond said, "You just want your due respect. I don't want the Wheaties [endorsement] and the Jordan stuff. You just want what you deserve."

Mitch Richmond has spent a lifetime scrambling for what he deserves, starting with the day his father walked out on Mitch and the family.

Chapter 2

Mitch Richmond was born on June 30, 1965. He was just four years old when his father decided to leave. Mitch never understood it, but he learned to live with it as he grew up in Fort Lauderdale, Florida.

"He wasn't bothered that much because I was always there for him," said his mother, Ernell O'Neal. (She remarried in 1988, which is why her last name is different from Mitch's.) "I was just like a mother and a father for him. He could always come to me and talk to me about anything. He often said he really didn't miss [his father] because I was always there for him."

But Mitch did miss his dad. His mother remembers a time in elementary school when each student was supposed to write a letter to his father. Mitch mailed his, but he never got a letter back.

"It just really bothered him that that he didn't have a response like the other kids," his mother admitted.

"I'm sure that in a perfect world, everyone has a mother and father right there," said Dana Altman, who coached Mitch at Moberly Area Junior College, in Moberly, Missouri, and at

Kansas State. "But I think Mitch got such great support from Ernell and Emma that I'm not sure he missed anything."

Emma Thomas was Mitch's grandmother. When Ernell had to work, Mitch's grandmother took care of him. She took him to the park. She listened to his problems. She became one of his best friends.

Ernell O'Neal said, "She [Emma Thomas] was the most sweetest, generous person you'd ever want to meet. And Mitch, sometimes I think he had some of her strength in him. She always told him to do his best. She always told him to put God first and everything else would be added."

His family didn't have much money, but Mitch didn't care. "It wasn't deep poverty," he said. "We weren't rich and we weren't poor, put it that way. But that's two good people that stayed with me. Some people feel that they have to have a dad around, but my mom was always there for me."

Meanwhile, his friends were telling him to play Florida's most popular sport, football. "All the way up through ninth

A young Mitch, and his mother, Ernell O'Neal (then Ernell Thomas), pose for a picture.

grade, that's where you could find me, out on the football field," Richmond said. "In Florida, football is big. It's really *the* game, the one that everybody cares about the most. They just seem to breed football players there."

Mitch had four friends from home who later played in the NFL: Michael Irvin, Brian Blades, Benny Blades, and Brett Perriman. But Richmond decided football practice was too physical, so he switched to basketball.

Julius Erving, nicknamed "Dr. J," was his idol, and like the good doctor, Mitch was a natural at the game. He was bigger than most of his friends, and he dominated them on the court. But he also lost interest in school. His family moved away from Fort Lauderdale, and Mitch started skipping classes. He wanted to play on the basketball team at Deerfield Beach High School, but the coach told him he wasn't good enough. As a freshman, he skipped so many classes that his mother decided to move him back to Fort Lauderdale.

Mitch wouldn't go to class at Fort Lauderdale's Boyd Anderson High School, either. One school administrator remembers him as being lazy. Mitch finally started to see things differently when he tried to join Boyd Anderson's basketball team.

"He came in the gym and said that he wanted to play basketball," said Jim Polk, the head coach. "I told him, 'First of all, you need to get into school.' And he said he didn't like to go to school because all he wanted to do was play basketball. And I told him, 'Well, I don't know whether you've come to the right place or not. You're going to have to go to class if you go here.'"

Mitch kept skipping classes. Polk often had to drive to Mitch's house and take him to school. At home, Ernell preached the value of an education, but Mitch was more worried about when Michael Jordan would be on TV.

"He wasn't dumb," Polk said. "You just had to stay on him all the time. When he studied, he didn't have any problems."

"A lot of kids there were trying to pull him down," Polk said. "I told him, 'Mitch, you can't soar with the eagles in the daytime if you fly with buzzards at night. You've got to be able to keep a step above them because if you don't, people are going to try to bring you down.'"

Finally, Ernell used basketball as a way to get Mitch into the classroom. He was watching Jordan on TV when she said to him, "You could become a basketball player. Is that what you want to do? You could become a Michael Jordan. Don't you ever think that any person could become something and you can't."

Ernell laughed when she remembered the story. "I was always telling him things like that, that he could become whatever he wanted to be," she said. "You want to become a basketball player?' I said. 'You can become one, but I can't do it for you. You have to get in the classroom and apply yourself and get your [college] degree.'"

College was the farthest thing from Mitch's mind, but he had no other choice if he wanted to play professional basketball. It was the early 1980s, before Shawn Kemp, Kobe Bryant, and Tracy McGrady had gone from high school to the NBA. To play in the NBA, Mitch would have to go to class and get better grades. If he didn't, he wouldn't be playing anywhere but the playground.

So Mitch hit the books. He went to summer school and night school to catch up. He even took a cooking class for credit. He started hanging out with Irvin, whom Polk remembers as being "a pretty good kid." Irvin used to drive Mitch home from school each night because Mitch didn't have a car.

Mitch played three years for Boyd Anderson's varsity, and the team went 65–17. Three of his teammates were so good that they later played professional basketball in Europe and the CBA, which is the NBA's minor leagues. But the star of the team was Mitch. He was even named a High School All-American.

"He would get distraught when you'd take him out of the game," Polk said. "He wanted to be in on every play."

As Mitch got closer to graduation, colleges started to call him. Kentucky wanted him. So did Texas A&M, Arkansas, and Providence, which was then coached by Rick Pitino.

"Every night, somebody [called]," Polk said. "Rick Pitino, he'd call every other day. [Mitch] stuck out like a sore thumb. He could do everything. I played him at forward and guard because I knew when he got to college he wasn't big enough to play as a center. We just wore him out. He averaged about 31 points a game."

But Mitch was still behind in his schoolwork. His grades were suddenly important, and he practiced marching down the aisle to get his diploma. But his grades were slightly below a C average, and the skipped classes finally caught up with him in his senior year.

In that season's final regular-season game, he sprained his ankle so badly that he had to miss the state playoffs. The team lost in the state championship game. More important, Mitch also missed an algebra test. His teacher refused to let him make it up, so he finished the year half a credit short of graduating. The only way Mitch could earn his degree was by taking a three-week course in summer school.

"He was really, really hurt because he wanted to march with his class, and he said to me, 'I'm not going to school anymore,'" Ernell said.

"Oh, yes, you are," she told him. "You go to this three-week class, and you show this teacher that you mean to become something in life. You don't let anybody stop you from

Principal Groom hands Mitch his first diploma.

reaching your goal. You've got a $100,000 scholarship that could be waiting for you; you're not going to throw that away."

Polk pushed Mitch, too. He told Mitch that if he got his diploma, he would eventually make more money than anybody else in the whole school, including the algebra teacher. "You'll change your name to Rich Man if you'll listen to what we tell you to do," Polk told Mitch.

So Mitch went to summer school, with Ernell driving him every morning to make sure he got there. But when he received his diploma, most colleges had already handed out their scholarships. Mitch also needed to keep pushing himself in the classroom. So instead of going to a national basketball power-house, Mitch went to Moberly Area Junior College in Moberly, Missouri. And as hard as it had been for him to get his high school diploma, adjusting to life at Moberly was even harder.

Chapter 3

Moberly Area Junior College was a shock to Richmond in many ways. It was an obscure junior college in what seemed like the middle of nowhere. A junior college (juco) is designed for students who don't have the opportunity to attend a four-year school. Many athletes go to junior college to improve their grades to become eligible for bigger schools.

But playing in Moberly wasn't part of Richmond's dream. He was used to the sunshine and warmth of Fort Lauderdale; Moberly is in central Missouri, where winters are cold and snowy. He was also used to lots of people; 150,000 people live in Fort Lauderdale, which also attracts more than 6 million tourists a year. Few people pick Moberly when planning their vacations.

But the biggest adjustment was being away from home. He arrived in Moberly in August 1984, a few weeks before school started. The dormitories weren't open yet, so he stayed in the basement of Dana Altman's house. Altman, the head coach at Moberly, didn't hesitate to open his home to Richmond.

"In talking with him on the phone a number of times, I just

really liked his personality and the way he handled himself," Altman said. "He was very easy-going, very respectful of people. He was always smiling and always upbeat, and people gravitated toward him."

But Richmond was unhappy in the dorms. He often called Altman in the middle of the night to say he was leaving. Each time, Altman invited him over and talked him into staying.

"The first year, we had a lot of those," Altman said with a chuckle. "He was a long way from home, and he got homesick bad that first year. The first couple of times it got real cold in Missouri, he wasn't used to that, either."

"Mitch told me, 'Ma, I used to stand and look down the road [toward home],'" Ernell said. "He wanted to come home. Dana would take Mitch to his house, and Mitch would play with his kids like Mitch was one of his children. [Dana] would tell him, 'Mitch, you can do it. Just stick it out.' And when Mitch called me, I would be telling him the same thing."

"He was a fine young man," Altman said, "and I knew that if he just gave it some time that he would mature and adjust to it. But I never really gave him that option [of going home]. He was going to have to find his own way home if he was going."

Richmond had to make an adjustment on the court, too. He was comfortable playing near the basket, like a center or power forward. But few power forwards in college basketball are six-feet five-inches tall, so Altman moved Richmond to shooting guard.

"You've got to improve your ball-handling skills," Altman said about the move to guard. "They just ask you to do a lot of different things: facing the basket, getting the ball to open people. The ball skills, the passing skills, the outside jumper have all got to improve. Mitch worked very hard his freshman year to make those things happen. It didn't happen all at once for him. He wasn't a big scorer his freshman year. He worked at doing a lot of other things."

And he helped Moberly win. With Richmond averaging 10.4 points per game, Moberly finished 35–5 and at one point in the season was ranked as high as third in the nation among junior colleges. The next season, Richmond averaged 16 points a game and was named the Region 16 Junior College Player of the Year. He was a first-team Juco All-American, and he was named to the National Juco All-Star Team. Moberly was ranked first in the country for most of the season until one of its stars, Charlie Bledsoe, broke his wrist late in the year. Still, Moberly finished 34–4 and sixth in the polls. Its 69–9 two-year record was its best ever.

But Altman kept pushing Mitch to do well in the class-room, too. He often asked, "Mitch, if you don't get a degree, what are you going to do for the next 40 years of your life?"

"When we started talking about this his freshman year, pro ball was just a dream," Altman said. "You wouldn't have the idea that he's going to be a lock for a first-round [NBA] draft choice and a pro. It was a reality check. Mitch had to realize that basketball may not be there for him his whole life. He needed to prepare himself for life after hoops."

"I was very impressed with the way he worked with his tutors and worked with all of his instructors in trying to catch up," Altman said. "He realized he'd cut some corners in high school and had to make up the time somewhere. I really thought he put that effort in at Moberly."

With good grades, Richmond could choose any Division I college he wanted, but he turned away the big-name schools. He chose Kansas State (K-State), located in Manhattan, Kansas. K-State was a weak team in the Big Eight Conference, but Richmond went there mainly because Altman was offered a job there as an assistant coach. Two of Richmond's

Moving along the baseline, Mitch Richmond dribbles around the
Wichita State defender. After completing his two years at Moberly Area
Community College, Richmond chose to attend Kansas State University.

teammates, Bledsoe and Fred McCoy, also followed Altman to K-State.

Altman said Richmond didn't have any problems adjusting to life in Kansas, but that was because Richmond managed to hide his homesickness from his coaches.

"He was even worse when he went to Kansas [State University]," Ernell O'Neal said. "He had a roommate, Bledsoe, and they used to call me, and he would say, 'Mom, I've got to leave here.' But I knew that in order for him to become something, I had to just keep that positive thinking and let him know that he had my support and my love and he could just make it. He could become whatever [he wanted]."

What Richmond became was one of the best players in college basketball. As a junior, he averaged 18.6 points and was named Second Team All-Big Eight. He scored 34 points to lead the K-State Wildcats past Georgia in the first round of the 1987 NCAA Tournament. The team lost in the second round to UNLV, but Richmond impressed enough people to earn a spot on the United States team for the World University Games in Zagreb, Yugoslavia. He led the United States in scoring in six of its eight games, and the team won the silver medal.

"He already knew he was a good player," said Steve Henson, then the point guard for K-State, "and then he got surrounded by what's supposed to be the elite of the country. He did such a good job with them. He saw that he was certainly an All-American type, one of the best players in the country."

With Richmond carrying the load, K-State was supposed to be a great team in the 1987–88 season. But Head Coach Lon Kruger started the year with a style that defended full-court and ran the fast break whenever possible. The Wildcats struggled through December with a 7–4 record, the last game of which was a 29-point loss to Purdue.

Kruger said the mood in the locker room was "very

In 1987, Richmond was selected for the United States basketball team that would compete at the World University Games. Richmond is seated, the last man on the right.

somber, of course. Dejected. It was the last game prior to a brief Christmas break. We changed a lot over that break. Quite frankly, we were pressing and running and Mitch wasn't touching [the ball] enough. So we came out of Christmas break and basically said, 'OK, Mitch is going to touch it every time down.'"

Mitch Richmond did some thinking during the Christmas break, too. He said, "I knew I had to get us going because things weren't looking too good then," he said. "I went home for Christmas and thought about it, then came back and talked to [Kruger]. We talked about how I could be playing a lot better. I wasn't playing the best that I can. I had to establish myself as a leader."

In the first game after the break, Richmond scored 33 points to lead K-State to an upset of nationally ranked Oklahoma. He later scored 41 points at Oklahoma, setting the

Lloyd Noble Arena record for scoring by an opponent. He scored K-State's final nine points in a win against Oklahoma State. He scored 35 in an upset of archrival Kansas, snapping the Jayhawks' 55-game home winning streak. The game was played at Kansas University's home court, the Allen Fieldhouse, in Lawrence, Kansas.

"That's just a great atmosphere, of course, a very hostile environment for the opposing teams," Kruger said. "It was a very methodical, hard-nosed whipping in the second half. Mitch just picked everyone up and . . . did what he wanted to do. Kansas had no answer that day, and they don't feel like that very often after a game at Allen [Fieldhouse]."

"It's a great place to play," Henson said. "It's a great place to win, without a doubt. There's so many things involved with a rivalry like that. The two schools are so close. They're always singing those songs in there, and it's a pretty good feeling when you ride the bus back afterwards and you know they weren't singing them that day."

K-State beat Kansas again in the Big Eight Tournament, then was selected to play in the 1988 NCAA Tournament. The Wildcats rolled through La Salle and DePaul to set up a rematch with Purdue, the top-seeded team in the region. The Boilermakers were considered to be one of the top teams in the country, if not the best, and they had gained confidence from beating K-State so badly in December.

"We knew we were a different team," Altman said. "We didn't know if we were 29 points better."

"A lot of things had changed," Henson said. "We felt like we were a much better team at that point in the season than we were before. On the other hand, we also realized they were loaded. They were stacked. They were a great team."

Purdue showed that greatness right away, streaking to a 10–0 lead to start the game. Kruger quickly called a timeout to

25

calm his players. He told them to do the things they'd worked on in practice, to play the way they'd played since Christmas. And he repeated what had been K-State's game plan for two months: get the ball to Richmond.

K-State cut Purdue's lead to 43–34 by halftime, then took over the game in the second half. Richmond scored 27 points, and K-State had a 73–70 win.

"Mitch got us going," Altman said. "That was really a game that showed how far we had come that year, and Mitch played a great game there. Other than the 10–0 start that they jumped on us with, we played a heck of a ballgame."

The Wildcats weren't ready to relax. If they won once more, they would go to the Final Four in Kansas City. But in what might have been the most important game in school history, K-State had to face archrival Kansas again.

"We felt great going into it," Henson said. "After beating Purdue, we felt like we had beaten clearly the best team in the region. And we had just beaten Kansas in the Big Eight Tournament. So we were confident that it was a team we could beat."

But there's a saying in college basketball that it's hard to beat the same team three times in a season. There's too much talent spread throughout the country. No school has enough scholarships to attract all the best players. Kansas's best player was senior Danny Manning, but he was surrounded by players that many people thought couldn't win a national title. Someone called the team Danny and the Miracles, a nickname that stuck. And the Jayhawks played miraculously that night against K-State.

Everywhere Richmond went, he was followed by at least two Jayhawks. They tried to keep the ball from him. When he managed to get the ball, Richmond either had to pass or to take a tough shot.

But K-State still led with 14:30 left in the game. Their defense collapsed on Manning, and he only scored two points the rest of the way. But Richmond had trouble scoring, too, and Kansas pulled away for a 71–58 win. Kansas went on to win the national championship; K-State just went home.

"That's got to be the toughest loss I'd ever experienced," Henson said. "I walked off to a different part of the locker room [and cried]."

"Losing a game to get to the Final Four was bad enough," Altman said, "but to lose to Kansas was even worse. That was a tough ballgame. We just ran out of gas down the stretch, and they got us."

One of the players who ran out of gas was Richmond. Harassed by Milt Newton and the other Jayhawks, Richmond

Trying to get off the shot, Mitch Richmond of Kansas State is surrounded by two University of Kansas defenders.

made just 4 of 14 shots and scored 11 points. Meanwhile, Newton had 18 points, 9 rebounds, and 7 assists.

"They didn't do anything different against me," said a disappointed Richmond. "They double-teamed me most of the time. Newton is a good, physical player, and he did a good job on me."

Looking back, though, the Wildcats had a great year. They tied the school record for wins in a season, with 25. They also made the Elite Eight for the first time since 1981.

Richmond did well, too. He averaged 22.6 points and was named a Second Team All-American by *The Sporting News* and *Basketball Weekly*. He caught the eye of NBA scouts. United States Olympic coach John Thompson picked him for the 1988 Olympic team. Richmond was going to have a chance to play for his country and then in the NBA. He'd achieved a lifelong dream.

But first, he had to live out his other dream. He'd earned enough credits to graduate from K-State. He would finally be able to walk down the aisle and receive his diploma.

Chapter 4

Mitch Richmond's mother, Ernell O'Neal, could hardly wait for graduation day.

"I was so overwhelmed because I knew that for the first time that I would see him walk down the aisle and get his degree," Ernell said. "To be able to think back to where he started from and where he ended up, I knew this would be the most exciting day of my life."

"When he put his mind to something, he was going to get it done," Altman said. "That really shows Mitch's character. He showed it at Moberly when he had to work awfully hard to catch up. And when he went to Kansas State, he did the same thing. He worked awfully hard to make sure that he graduated on time."

"As much as he wanted to play in the NBA, he wanted that degree," Kruger said. "So many times, young people that know they're going to play in the NBA stop going to school and stop really applying themselves. That wasn't the case with Mitch at all."

Ernell was determined not to miss the graduation. She got

As he grew older, Richmond learned the value of a college education. He worked hard at Kansas State and graduated with his senior class.

into the family car with her new husband, Joseph O'Neal, and drove for two days to see Richmond receive his Bachelor of Arts degree in Social Sciences.

The end of college was just the beginning of the most hectic summer of Richmond's life. He was invited to attend the NBA draft in late June. He was also busy with the Olympic team, which spent the summer practicing and playing exhibition games leading up to the Olympics in Seoul. Sometimes, Richmond was overwhelmed by it all. He told Ernell, "Mom, everything is going so fast."

Richmond also played in the Orlando All-Star Classic, a weeklong camp for possible NBA draft picks. Scouts watched the players closely, trying to decide who would help their teams. Some scouts thought Richmond was a "tweener," meaning someone whose size leaves him between positions. Was Richmond too small to play forward? Was he too big to play guard?

Bob Lanier didn't care where Richmond played. A star

center for the Detroit Pistons and Milwaukee Bucks from 1970–84, Lanier said, "If [Mitch] doesn't make it in the pros, I'll eat my shoes." Lanier's shoes were size twenty-one.

Richmond won over any doubters in Orlando. Stu Inman, the player personnel director of the Miami Heat, said, "He was in good shape coming in. He's in much better shape now. If everything went wrong for Mitch Richmond in the draft, he stills goes [in the top 10 picks]."

Richmond tried not to let the hype get to him. For example, while the other players invited their girlfriends to the draft, he asked his mom to go. She said no because she was afraid to fly in an airplane.

But Ernell quickly changed her mind. She told herself, "Here's a child. I raised him up. He became somebody that graduated from college, and here he's about to enter another step [in life]. I can never let him go alone."

The draft was held in New York, and with Ernell, Richmond flew there from Florida. "I was so nervous," she said. "He's holding my hand on the airplane. Mitch got a blanket, covered up and went to sleep. And every time he'd wake up, I was still looking out the window. And he would say to me, 'Mom, are you all right?'"

At the draft, Richmond waited anxiously for his name to be called. His agent thought he might drop in the draft, costing him money; the quicker a player is drafted, the more money he makes. The Los Angeles Clippers took Danny Manning with the first pick. Then the Indiana Pacers drafted seven-foot four-inch Rik Smits from Marist College. The Clippers picked again at No. 3 and selected Charles Smith from the University of Pittsburgh, and the New Jersey Nets took Auburn's Chris Morris.

Richmond knew he wouldn't be picked fifth. That pick belonged to the Golden State Warriors, who needed a center more than anything else.

The Warriors surprised everyone by taking Mitch Richmond.

Golden State's head coach and general manager, Don Nelson, had been in the NBA as a player, coach, or GM since 1962. He'd won five championships as a player for the Boston Celtics. He'd coached the Milwaukee Bucks before taking over in Golden State, and he knew Richmond was the player he wanted.

"I believe that whenever possible, you should draft star quality," Nelson said. "And we think Mitch Richmond has star quality."

Richmond did not have much time to think about where he was selected. He spent the summer getting ready for the Olympics. The team included David Robinson, then a naval officer who later starred for the San Antonio Spurs; Manning; North Carolina's J. R. Reid; Georgetown's point guard, a different Charles Smith from the one drafted by the Clippers; UNLV's Stacey Augmon; Georgia's Willie Anderson; Western Michigan's Dan Majerle; and Bradley's Hersey Hawkins.

The United States Men's Basketball Team was coming off a losing year in 1987; Brazil had upset the Americans in the Pan-American Games in Indianapolis. There was a lot of pressure on Richmond and his teammates to bring home the gold.

The team played a series of exhibition games against NBA players in August. The goal was to give the Olympic players some experience together before leaving for Seoul. One of those exhibitions took place in Las Vegas, and the NBA team was coached by Don Nelson. He met with Richmond before the game, and Richmond was shocked by what he heard.

"Everyone told me that Nelson was tough on rookies, that he didn't even like rookies," Richmond said. "I didn't really believe them. And then I met Don in Las Vegas. He told me that not many rookies had ever played for him. He told me he didn't

The 1988 Kansas State Wildcats. Richmond is in the back row, fourth from the right. After the college basketball season was over, Richmond was chosen to play for the United States Olympic Basketball Team, set to compete in Seoul, South Korea.

like rookies. It was mind-boggling. I didn't know what to think."

Richmond was just as confused by his experience in Seoul. The United States didn't make it to the gold medal game for the first time in Olympic history. Richmond and his teammates settled for a bronze medal that felt like lead in their hearts because they had expected so much more. It was also the last time the United States sent a team of college players to the Olympics. Using the disappointing finish as their reason, USA Basketball voted to send professionals from then on. In 1992, Michael Jordan, Magic Johnson, and Larry Bird led the first Dream Team to the gold in Barcelona, Spain. Meanwhile, Richmond lived with the bitterness of the loss.

"I had a great time playing with some of the greatest players in the world," he said. "But I felt we should have won, no doubt about it."

33

Chapter 5

There was a lot for Richmond to like about Golden State. The team played in Oakland, California, which meant no more Kansas blizzards. An NBA legend was his head coach. The Warriors already had All-Star guard Chris Mullin, who never seemed to miss a shot.

But the Warriors had a lot to prove. In a chaotic season the year before, Head Coach George Karl resigned in March because the team refused to give him a contract extension. Golden State finished 20–62, and few people expected the team to improve.

Richmond fit in right away. He played so well in training camp that Nelson changed his mind about rookies. He moved Mullin to small forward so Richmond could start at shooting guard.

"He wasn't like most rookies," said teammate Terry Teagle. "He believed in himself and he knew he belonged in this league. I haven't seen someone come into the NBA with that much composure since Michael Jordan."

"From the day he walked in as a rookie, he was a guy you

could count on to give you two things: about 20 points a night and every ounce of effort he had," said Golden State assistant coach Garry St. Jean. "And he would do it without ever once calling attention to himself."

Richmond was well known for his work ethic in college, and Mullin was just as dedicated. Mullin was a gym rat, the kind of player who showed up before noon for a night game. His practice routine included taking five hundred shots every morning between 7:30 and 8:00.

"I finally found someone who was in the gym before me," Richmond said. "I thought I had a good work ethic, but Chris worked even harder than I did."

The new friends pushed each other all season, and the Warriors' record improved to 43–39. Mullin averaged 26.5 points, and Richmond averaged 22.5. Along the way, Richmond scored 47 in a game against Sacramento and was named NBA Rookie of the Month three times. He joined Hall of Famers Wilt Chamberlain and Rick Barry as the only Warrior rookies to average at least 20 points.

Mullin was so impressed that he gave Richmond the nickname Rock, as in "rock steady." That nickname has stuck with him ever since.

Golden State made the playoffs for just the second time in twelve years, then upset heavily favored Utah, 3–0, in the first round. They used a small, quick lineup built around Richmond and Mullin. The Warriors lost to Phoenix, 4–1, in the second round of the playoffs, but it was a successful year.

After the season, Richmond was named the 1988–89 NBA Rookie of the Year. "Mitch established himself as one of the top impact rookies in my years," Nelson said. "It's such a pleasure to have someone who is so very talented and who is willing to play a team game. There's nothing, nothing he didn't do for us this year."

In the 1988 NBA draft, Mitch Richmond was selected fifth overall by the Golden State Warriors.

Richmond thanked his mother for making the award possible. "She was there when I needed her," he said. "When I wanted to do something, she always told me to go out and grab it."

But Richmond wasn't satisfied. "Mental preparation is something I'd like to improve on," he said. "Seeing the floor better, touching up my physical tools. I've got to react quicker, think things out. Oh, yeah, there's room for improvement."

Golden State had room for improvement, too. They needed a big player to go with Richmond and Mullin. But in the 1989 draft, Nelson surprised everybody again. He drafted point guard Tim Hardaway and again committed the Warriors to up-tempo basketball.

It was an exciting style to watch. During the 1989–90 season, the Warriors led the NBA in team scoring for the first time in fourteen seasons, averaging 116.3 points. Mullin averaged 25.1 and made the All-Star team. Hardaway averaged 14.7 points and 8.7 assists; he was named to the league's All-Rookie team. Richmond didn't receive any postseason honors, but he averaged 22.1 points, 4.6 rebounds, and 2.9 assists.

Because of the success of Richmond and Hardaway, Nelson admitted to a change of heart about rookies. "I don't really hate rookies," he said. "I just wish they were older and smarter."

Richmond, Mullin, and Hardaway became stars off the court, too. A local newspaper ran a contest to give them a nickname. Among the ideas were The Totally Tubular Trio, The Joint Chiefs of Stats, and The Three That Be. But the winner was a takeoff on the name of the popular rap group Run DMC. They became Run TMC, for the first initials of their names (Tim, Mitch, and Chris).

But the Warriors were still too small. They were outrebounded in 71 of their 82 games. Their record dropped to

37–45, and they set an NBA record for the fewest offensive rebounds per game with an average of 11.2.

Richmond and his mates did their best to overcome their shortcomings the next season, 1990–91. They started the year 11–6 and finished fourth in the Pacific Division, with a record of 44–38.

Of course, Run TMC led the way. Mullin averaged 25.7 points, good for eighth in the league; Richmond averaged 23.9, good for tenth; and Hardaway's 22.9 was eleventh. The team averaged 116.6 points, its highest total since the 1967–68 season.

Again, Mullin made the All-Star team. So did Hardaway. But Richmond was left off the team again. He shrugged it off, saying, "I can't do anything about it now. I don't have any control over how people judge what I've been doing. I just have to go out and keep doing it." The next night, Richmond blitzed the Los Angeles Clippers with 40 points, 7 rebounds, and 7 assists.

Golden State faced the San Antonio Spurs in the first round of the 1991 playoffs. Using the same run-and-gun style that beat Utah two years earlier, the Warriors upset the Spurs, 3–1. But they were drubbed again in the second round, this time 4–1 by the Lakers, and Nelson again worried his team was too small and too reliant on Run TMC.

Golden State was only the sixteenth team in NBA history to have three players average at least 20 points per game, but none of those teams ever won an NBA title. The Warriors had been outrebounded in sixty regular-season games. In the playoffs, they couldn't stop the Lakers' taller players like Kareem Abdul-Jabbar, Magic Johnson, and James Worthy. If the Warriors were going to contend for a championship, they had to get bigger.

But acquiring players in the NBA is hard to do. The league

With the Warriors, Richmond was one of the featured players in a high-scoring offense. Richmond, Chris Mullin, and Tim Hardaway were known around the league as Run TMC because of their fast-paced style of play.

has a salary cap that limits the money each team can pay its players. The salary cap is designed to keep a few teams from signing all the good players, but it also makes it hard for mediocre teams to sign better players. Nelson's only option was to trade one of his three stars.

On the first day of the 1991–92 season, just hours before the Warriors' first game, Nelson announced that he'd made a trade. Richmond and teammate Les Jepsen were going to the Sacramento Kings for Billy Owens.

Chapter 6

Sacramento is where NBA players go to die. At least, it seemed that way to Richmond. The Kings had won just 25 games the previous year. They managed to win only one road game the entire year. Their last championship was in 1951 when they were the Rochester (New York) Royals. They had not made the playoffs since 1986, and they weren't going to make the playoffs in 1991–92, either.

Sacramento drafted Billy Owens from Syracuse with the third overall pick in the 1991 draft. Owens was a six-foot nine-inch forward with the skills of a guard, and NBA scouting director Marty Blake predicted that Owens would be an All-Star within three years. But Owens refused to play in Sacramento. He threatened to sit out the season so another team could take him in the next draft. Faced with losing Owens anyway, the Kings traded him for whatever they could get.

What they got was a prize player coveted by many teams. Richmond was coming into his own, and the Kings saw him as the player around whom they could build a team.

But the Kings weren't very good at doing that. In the 1985 draft, for example, they drafted Joe Kleine instead of Chris Mullin. In 1986, they took Kenny Smith when future All-Star Kevin Johnson was available. In 1989, they took Pervis Ellison with the first pick in the draft, ignoring future All-Stars Sean Elliott and Glen Rice. And in 1991, they picked Owens instead of future stars Dikembe Mutombo, Steve Smith, and Terrell Brandon.

"The league decides what players it's gonna make famous," said Kings center Olden Polynice. "It's nobody who's *here*. If you got sent here, you are in exile."

That might sound harsh, but Richmond felt the same way. He was crushed by the trade and immediately called Dana Altman.

"He either called from the airport or from the plane, and he was really down," Altman said. "Mitch had a tendency to get pretty close with his coaches. He really liked Coach Nelson, and when he was traded, it really hurt him. I think that was the first time he realized that basketball was a business. It was the first time a coach had ever let him go. He really had a hard time understanding [why]."

"That was, I think, the worst day," said his mother. "He was so down. He had gotten so used to being at Golden State with Chris and Tim that it really, really bothered him."

"Boom! I'm in Sacramento!" Richmond said. "Sacramento? Is that an NBA team? . . . You thought you were with a *team* [at Golden State]. Happy-go-lucky. Having a good time with the guys. I didn't realize the business side. Then it hit me."

His mother had tried to prepare Richmond for the possibility. She'd told him that playing in the NBA was a job. "Wherever your job takes you, you've got to go," she told him. But her message didn't sink in until Richmond called to tell

In 1991, Richmond was traded to the Sacramento Kings for Billy Owens. He was sad to leave his Warriors teammates.

her about the trade. He was sad, and Ernell did her best to cheer him up.

"God does everything for a reason," she told Richmond. "You might not see it right now, but somewhere down the line you're going to be happy. Plenty of young men would love to be in your shoes to play anywhere in the NBA. You still have your job."

Mitch Richmond reported to the Kings, but he refused to move to Sacramento. Instead, he drove eighty miles from Oakland every day, then drove the eighty miles home. "He wasn't the same for quite a while," said his wife, Juli, a former model whom he'd met during his rookie season and married two years later.

Richmond did his best on the court, though. He was ninth

in the league in scoring with an average of 22.5 points per game. He also became the Kings' go-to player at the end of the game; only Michael Jordan and Karl Malone scored more points in the fourth quarter than Richmond did.

But the team didn't fare well. It finished last in the Pacific Division, with a record of 29–53. Head Coach Dick Motta was fired halfway through the season. Richmond noticed that his new teammates "didn't seem to be working as hard as I was used to working."

Meanwhile, Golden State improved with Owens. As Richmond watched longingly from Sacramento, his former teammates won 55 games. Owens averaged 14.3 points, 8.0 rebounds, and 2.4 assists. He also made 52.5 percent of his shots. The Warriors didn't seem to miss Richmond at all.

During the off-season, Sacramento hired Golden State assistant coach Garry St. Jean as its new head coach. "When you're an assistant [coach], you aspire to any [head coaching] job," St. Jean said. "But to have Mitch Richmond here is special to me because of the relationship we have. He's going to have a great year."

Almost overnight, Richmond was excited about the upcoming 1992–93 season. St. Jean's hiring put Richmond's former teammates at ease, too.

"I know [the trade] was tough on Mitch," Mullin said, "but it was tough on me, too. The timing was tough. I'm just glad things have worked out as well as they have. Saint has really stabilized things up there, and Mitch looks really good, really sharp."

"Saint's up there with him," Hardaway said. "Family's up there with him. That's how I look at it. With Saint there, they'll be better."

In the first half of the season, Richmond played the best basketball of his career so far. He averaged 21.9 points and was selected as a reserve to the All-Star Game. He also accepted the trade.

"Now I feel it was for the best," he said. "It was a trade, and it was tough. [But] people go through tough times and can't feed their families. I don't want to say I was so sick I couldn't eat or anything like that. I tried to do the best job I could last year. I had to adjust, and I think I adjusted pretty well. I'm very proud of how I handled the situation."

Richmond signed a five-year contract extension, which would make him a King through the 1998–99 season. He thought the Kings would be good enough to win an NBA title in a few years, and he wanted to be a part of it. The Kings were glad to have him, too.

"You'd have to put him at the top of the group right behind Michael Jordan and Clyde Drexler [at shooting guard]," said Kings general manager Jerry Reynolds. "The thing I like about Mitch is that he studies the game. Basketball is his life."

But the team struggled again, mainly because of injuries. Just two days after being named an All-Star for the first time, Richmond broke a thumb. He missed not only the All-Star Game but the rest of the season, too.

Before the 1993–94 season, Richmond finally moved his family to Sacramento. He was ready to help turn the Kings into a winner. Everything looked good when Sacramento drafted Bobby Hurley to help get the ball to Richmond. Hurley won two NCAA championships as the point guard at Duke, and his gritty style would fit well with Richmond's game.

But whatever momentum the Kings had gathered was smashed nineteen games into the season. Hurley's car was hit by another car that was driving at night without headlights, and he almost died. Hurley missed the rest of the season, and though he came back the next year, his game has never been the same.

That accident took the life out of the Kings, too. They finished the season in a familiar way—a 28–54 record and near the bottom of the division. Richmond had another banner year, though. He was named to the All-NBA second team, and with Michael Jordan cruising the highways of minor-league baseball, Richmond led all guards in scoring with an average of 23.4 points.

Many people expected Richmond to be named to Dream Team II, which was to play in the 1994 World Championships in Toronto that summer. The head coach was Don Nelson, and Richmond had proven himself to be the top shooting guard in the league. But he wasn't invited to play. The United States won easily, but along the way the players were criticized for taunting opponents, talking too much trash, and celebrating too much after dunks. Ironically, Richmond was one of the most well-behaved players in the whole NBA.

Richmond's breakout year was the next one, 1994–95. He scored the ten thousandth point of his career in December. He was again the top scoring guard in the league, and he was named to the All-Star Game as a reserve for the second time.

That All-Star Game was held in the America West Arena in Phoenix. Richmond dominated the third quarter, scoring 10 points. He made 10 of 13 shots in the game and finished with 23 points. He was named the game's Most Valuable Player, and his West team blew out the East, 139–112.

While Richmond was being interviewed after the game, Charles Barkley sneaked up and kissed him on the neck. Barkley said with a smile, "We can trade for you, too."

But Richmond was happy in Sacramento. The Kings finally had a winning record, 25–20, and were on pace to make the playoffs. Their defense had improved greatly; they allowed almost eight points fewer per game than the previous year.

"[That] was the first year that Mitch looked like he was glad to be here," said Sacramento teammate Lionel Simmons.

But the Kings collapsed down the stretch. They were 14–23 after the All-Star break, dropping into a tie with the Denver Nuggets for the Western Conference's final playoff spot. On the last day of the season, Sacramento played Denver in a winner-take-all game. The winner would go to the play-offs. The loser would go home. The Nuggets won.

Adding to Richmond's disappointment was the death of his grandmother, Emma. "When Mitch was growing up, we were at every game he played at high school," Ernell said. "My mom was there. She used to stand up and take off her jacket and swing it around. She would say, 'Stop giving the ball away now!' And when my mom died, Mitch said, 'Mom, I just can't see going in the arena playing and Granny is not in the stands.'"

But Richmond did return to the arena. The next year, 1995–96, he was eighth in NBA scoring with an average of 23.1. But the most important thing he did was to lead the Kings to the promised land, the NBA playoffs, for the first time since 1986.

The Kings started the year as one of the most impressive teams in the West, going 19–9. They were in first place in the Pacific Division. But they faded in the second half of the sea-son. They managed to hold off Denver and Golden State for the last Western Conference playoff spot, but they lost in the first round to Seattle, 3–1.

Richmond's success earned him another shot at an Olympic gold medal. Prior to the season, USA Basketball had named ten of the twelve players who would be on Dream Team III for the 1996 Summer Olympics in Atlanta. Richmond was added to the team in the spring, but not until all of the Dream Team T-shirts, lunch boxes, and action figures had

During the 1995–96 season, Richmond led the Kings to the playoffs. Though Sacramento lost in the first round, it was the first time in ten years that the team had been involved in postseason play.

already been produced. While his Olympic teammates attracted the attention of souvenir buyers, Richmond was left out.

But he tried to understand it. "I'm not the high-flying dunker or anything fancy," he said. "Maybe my game isn't what they want for the commercials and TV appearances. It bothered me a little when I was younger, but I don't worry about it anymore. If the recognition comes, it comes. If not, I'll just keep doing what I've been doing."

That's exactly what he did during the Olympics. Richmond was one of the Dream Team's top scorers, and the United States easily won the gold medal. For him, it was redemption for America's failure in Seoul. After eight years of waiting, he finally had his gold medal. That beat having his own action figure any day.

Chapter 7

Mitch Richmond's mother and grandmother did a good job teaching him what's important in life.

"He was brought up right," said Richmond's high school coach, Jim Polk. "He's always even keel. He treats people right."

"He is such a loving, caring, wonderful person off the court," Ernell said. "He's just a wonderful young man, a wonderful son to have. I always tell him, 'Mitch, always try to treat everybody right. You have to be good to other people's kids because one day somebody might have to be good to your kids.'"

Juli and Mitch's first child, Phillip, was born in 1993. Their second son, Jerin, was born in 1995.

Although Richmond is away from home a lot during basketball season, he spends as much time with his kids as he can. When he returns from a long road trip, for example, he wakes them up no matter what time it is.

"(Juli) gets mad, but I can't help it," Mitch said. "I have to see them."

Richmond is also active in the community. He often made

public appearances for Sacramento's "Kings in the Community" charitable foundation. He's the cohost for an annual celebrity pool tournament. He's involved with the Pediatric Aids Foundation, Sacramento's Dayspring Outreach program for troubled youth, the United Way, the Make-A-Wish Foundation, and the University of California-Davis Hospital's Pediatrics Department. He has a special interest in raising money for UCD's sickle cell anemia research; two of his cousins have the disease.

Richmond also started a program in Fort Lauderdale to keep kids interested in school. His "SOLID AS A ROCK" Student-Athlete Program is open to boys and girls between ten and seventeen years old. Those students must be in an organized sports program and have a grade-point average of at least 2.7. The foundation supplies students with tickets to NBA games. It also offers college scholarships.

Richmond even helped out the state of California's Department of Recycling. He appeared in a commercial where he played a game of one-on-one with a blue-and-green dinosaur named Recycle Rex. Shooting plastic and aluminum drink bottles, Rex won the game, causing Richmond to ask for "best two out of three."

Richmond's friends and family describe him as laid-back, quiet, and fun-loving. He's a good bowler; he once scored a 215 (out of a possible 300). He likes playing EA Sports video games. During the summer of 1997, he also made his first acting appearance. He played a murder suspect on *The Sentinel*, seen on the UPN Network.

Richmond is also known for his impersonations of other players in the NBA. His impression of Miami's Alonzo Mourning at the free-throw line earned a mention in *Sports Illustrated*. NBC's *Inside Stuff* also featured several of his impersonations.

Getting ready for the next game, Mitch Richmond puts the moves on teammate Olden Polynice.

"I'm telling you," Richmond said, "there's nobody in the league I can't do."

"Mitch can be hilarious," said Garry St. Jean, his former coach. "For the team Christmas party, we should just show a video of him imitating every guy in the league."

"He does me even better than I can do myself," said former teammate Chris Mullin.

Richmond made people laugh in college, too. "He was always one of those guys that his teammates enjoyed very much," Lon Kruger said. "He was able to keep them loose. He was a guy that didn't mind having a good time in a very healthy way."

"Anytime I'm down a little bit, I might pick up the phone and give [Mitch] a call because he's always pretty upbeat," Coach Altman said.

But memories of Richmond don't always involve jokes or three-point shots. "I had a couple of sons that were born when Mitchell played for me," Altman said. "[I remember] him going to see my wife at the hospital and him at the house just sitting around watching TV, watching film. Those were real special times on a personal note."

Coach Polk's favorite memories of Richmond involve the simplest things. Polk occasionally offered free hamburgers to any player who could hit fifty free throws in a row after practice; Richmond would try until 9:00 at night. Richmond also would ask, "Coach, can I hold a dollar?" when he wanted to buy something to eat.

"I saw him the summer [of 1996]," said Polk, "and I said, 'Well, man, I need to hold a dollar.'"

Richmond bought a house in southern Florida during the summer of 1997 because so many of his friends and family still lived there. One of his brothers was going to try out for the high school basketball team. His ten-year-old brother made the

53

Mitch Richmond is always trying to improve his game. Working hard in practice gives him an edge at game time.

All-Star team in his basketball league. His sister was in middle school. His mother was still there. Only his nineteen-year-old brother had moved away; he was majoring in psychology at Alabama State.

"He's the right kind of people," Polk said. "As far as I know, he never drank, never smoked cigarettes, never did dope. He's clean. I told Mitch I'm really proud of him for making all that money and playing in the NBA, but I was really proud of him for getting out of college because I saw where he came from. They were nice people and always clean, but he came a long way."

Chapter 8

Richmond did not think he had gone far enough. By midway through the 1996–97 season, he asked Sacramento for a trade. He didn't think the Kings had a chance to win an NBA championship during his career.

Richmond was also bothered that several other shooting guards had signed big contracts that dwarfed his $3.5 million per year salary. Jordan was getting $30 million. Reggie Miller was getting $10 million. Even Allan Houston was getting $9 million. At the 1997 All-Star Game, Richmond hinted he'd be sent to Miami before the trading deadline later in the month.

That trade never happened.

Late in the season, St. Jean was fired. The team missed the playoffs again. But it had been another great year for Richmond. He made the All-Star team for the fifth straight year. He averaged a career-high 25.9 points. He became just the seventh player ever to average at least 21 points in each of his first nine seasons. The others were Kareem Abdul-Jabbar, Rick Barry, Larry Bird, Wilt Chamberlain, Michael Jordan,

In 1997, Richmond asked the Kings to trade him. He wanted to play for a team that had a chance of winning the NBA title.

and Oscar Robertson; each of them was either in the Naismith Basketball Hall of Fame or destined to be there.

Richmond was desperate to play for a winning team. Over the summer, he again asked for a trade.

Rumors flew that Richmond wouldn't show up for training camp, that he would hold out until the Kings traded him. He reported to camp and started the season with the Kings, but his heart wasn't in playing for them. On the court, he hustled as hard as always; through the first twenty-one games of the 1997–98 season, Richmond was fourth in the league in scoring (22.9 points per game). But the trade rumors became a distraction for his teammates, four of whom were rookies.

The young players wanted to win, but Richmond did not necessarily want to be part of another rebuilding process. "They're playing hard, trying to learn, but they're definitely

56

young," Richmond said. "It's frustrating. I'm starting over again."

Off the court, Richmond's situation became a media circus. Before a game with the Knicks, Richmond held an impromptu press conference with New York reporters while his teammates warmed up. He appeared on ESPN's *The NBA Today* to say he wasn't being selfish. He let TNT conduct a live interview in his home to say he just cared about winning.

It wasn't a fun time for the Kings, either. General Manager Geoff Petrie spent so much time answering questions about Richmond that he had two signs made for his office door. One said, "Mitch Richmond has not been traded." The other said Richmond had.

People close to Richmond hoped he would be traded as soon as possible. They were convinced he'd never get the recognition he deserved if he stayed in Sacramento.

"I read statements by [Michael] Jordan and other players always talking about how good they think Mitch is," Altman said. "But the media, I don't know if they give him the credit that he's due. I am a little worried that he won't take his proper place in the history books because he never got the exposure. People like Jordan recognize him as one of the top guards. I wish he'd be recognized like that more often."

"I think about it a lot," Ernell said, "because I know he probably thinks about it. He is such a great player and he doesn't get the recognition, but you know what I say as a Christian woman? I always say God does it for a reason. Maybe it's not his time that he wants Mitch to shine. I feel like in time it's going to come. The windows are going to be open, and no one can close them."

"I always tell him, 'Mitch, you go out there and you do what you know to do with life. God will take care of the rest. If it's your time to move, to get traded, no one can hinder it if God is in the plan.'"

On May 14, 1998, Richmond and teammate Otis Thorpe were traded to the Washington Wizards for forward Chris Webber. By acquiring Richmond, the Wizards knew they were getting more than a great scorer. He also gave them a player with great leadership ability, something Washington lacked on its young team. With stars like Richmond, Juwan Howard, and Rod Strickland, the Wizards have a good chance of getting back to the playoffs.

Although he has left Sacramento, Richmond has a lot of memories to take with him, but none will mean more than his performance on December 21, 1996. Ernell was in town to visit, and Mitch gave her his Olympic gold medal. She wore it that night to the Kings' game against the Portland Trail Blazers.

Mitch Richmond still maintains a close relationship with his mom, Ernell O'Neal.

Rising in the air, Mitch Richmond looks to shoot over Chris Mullin and Dale Davis of the Indiana Pacers.

The game was close late in the fourth quarter. Richmond scored a basket to tie the game, then scored all of Sacramento's points in overtime. Despite Richmond's efforts, the game was still tied with 1.8 seconds left in overtime. The Kings had the ball out of bounds at midcourt.

Richmond lined up on the far side of the court, near the foul lane. The pass floated toward him, and he jumped to catch it. As he soared, he caught the ball and rolled his hand over in one motion. Over a defender's outstretched fingers, he rolled the ball off the backboard and through the net. The buzzer went off, and the crowd erupted. His mother jumped from her seat, clutched the gold medal, and cried.

Richmond finished the game with 37 points, 5 rebounds, and 5 assists. His teammates mobbed him on the floor. *SportsCenter* made sure it had the highlights for its 2:00 A.M. show.

"I'm praying for Mitch to get the last shot so it could go in to win, and I opened my eyes, and Mitchell hit it!" Ernell said. "It won the game, and I started to cry. It was so wonderful to be able to just sit there and witness that last shot that Mitch, that my son, had made for them to win that game."

But that was only as it should be. Mitch Richmond would never be where he is today without the support of his mother, and nobody understands that better than Richmond himself.

Career Statistics

College

YEAR	TEAM	GP	FG%	REB	AST	PTS	AVG
1984–85	Moberly Area	40	.480	185	98	415	10.4
1985–86	Moberly Area	38	.478	251	99	608	16.0
Junior College Totals		78	.479	436	197	1,023	13.1
1986–87	Kansas State	30	.447	170	80	559	18.6
1987–88	Kansas State	34	.514	213	125	768	22.6
4-year College Totals		64	.483	383	205	1,327	20.7

NBA

YEAR	TEAM	GP	FG%	REB	AST	STL	BLK	PTS	AVG
1988–89	Golden State	79	.468	468	334	82	13	1,741	22.0
1989–90	Golden State	78	.497	360	223	98	24	1,720	22.1
1990–91	Golden State	77	.494	452	238	126	34	1,840	23.9
1991–92	Sacramento	80	.468	319	411	92	34	1,803	22.5
1992–93	Sacramento	45	.474	154	221	53	9	987	21.9
1993–94	Sacramento	78	.445	286	313	103	17	1,823	23.4
1994–95	Sacramento	82	.446	357	311	91	29	1,867	22.8
1995–96	Sacramento	81	.447	269	255	125	19	1,872	23.1
1996–97	Sacramento	81	.454	319	338	118	24	2,095	25.9
1997–98	Sacramento	70	.445	229	279	88	15	1,623	23.2
Totals		751	.463	3,213	2,923	976	218	17,371	23.1

GP=Games played
AST=Assists
BLK=Blocks
STL=Steals

PTS=Total points scored
FG%=Field goal percentage
REB=Rebounds
AVG=Points per game

61

Where to Write Mitch Richmond:

Mr. Mitch Richmond
c/o Washington Wizards
MCI Center
601 F Street NW
Washington, DC 20071

On the Internet at:

http://www.nba.com/playerfile/mitch_richmond.html
http://www.nba.com/Wizards

Index